WITHDRAWN FROM LIBRARY

American Culture & Conflict

Living Through WORLD WAR II

M.M. Eboch

Educational Media
rourkeeducationalmedia.com

Before & After Reading Activities

Before Reading:

Building Academic Vocabulary and Background Knowledge

Before reading a book, it is important to tap into what your child or students already know about the topic. This will help them develop their vocabulary, increase their reading comprehension, and make connections across the curriculum.

1. Look at the cover of the book. What will this book be about?
2. What do you already know about the topic?
3. Let's study the Table of Contents. What will you learn about in the book's chapters?
4. What would you like to learn about this topic? Do you think you might learn about it from this book? Why or why not?
5. Use a reading journal to write about your knowledge of this topic. Record what you already know about the topic and what you hope to learn about the topic.
6. Read the book.
7. In your reading journal, record what you learned about the topic and your response to the book.
8. After reading the book complete the activities below.

Content Area Vocabulary

Read the list. What do these words mean?

- censors
- harassed
- humanity
- industry
- infamy
- internment
- mandated
- pollutant
- recruitment
- reforms
- segregated

After Reading:

Comprehension and Extension Activity

After reading the book, work on the following questions with your child or students in order to check their level of reading comprehension and content mastery.

1. How did the attack on Pearl Harbor change American attitudes about entering the war? (Summarize)
2. How did World War II help improve the U.S. economy? (Infer)
3. Why did the war increase opportunities for some groups but take away rights for other groups? (Asking Questions)
4. How can individuals help promote peace in their countries and worldwide? (Text to Self Connection)
5. What inventions that we use today were developed during World War II? (Asking Questions)

Extension Activity

A memorial is a structure that helps people remember a past event. Find pictures of some Holocaust memorials. Look also at the Pearl Harbor Historic Sites. How do these places help visitors remember those events? How do they educate people about the past? Design your own memorial. Encourage people to remember the Japanese internment camps. Then explore some of the existing memorials to the camps. How does yours compare?

TABLE OF CONTENTS

Poised for War 4
War Brings Change 12
Rights Expanded, Rights Destroyed 22
Suffering and Surviving 38
Lingering Effects 42
Glossary 46
Index 47
Show What You Know 47
Further Reading 47
About the Author 48

KEY EVENTS

1914 – 1918:	World War I
1929:	Great Depression begins in United States
September 1, 1939:	World War II begins
December 7, 1941:	Japanese bomb Pearl Harbor
December 8, 1941:	The U.S. declares war on Japan, entering World War II
December 11-13, 1941:	Nazi Germany and its Axis partners declare war on the U.S.
June 6, 1944:	American, British, and other Allied troops land on France's Normandy beaches, opening a second warfront against Germany
May 7, 1945:	Germany surrenders to western Allies
August 6, 1945:	U.S. drops atomic bomb on Japan
September 2, 1945:	Japan formally surrenders, World War II ends
1946:	Manhattan Project ends; last Japanese internment camp closes in U.S.
1948:	United Nations issues Universal Declaration of Human Rights

CHAPTER ONE

POISED FOR WAR

A war does not begin from nothing. Problems often build for years before the first battle. In the 1930s, tension had been building for two decades.

The world had already suffered through one major war. World War I ran from 1914 to 1918. After that war, the United States enjoyed a peaceful and prosperous decade. People thought the riches would last forever.

Yet hard times were coming.

More than 116,000 American military personnel died fighting in World War I.

AMERICANS FOR PEACE

How can people prevent war? Around the world, Peace Societies—groups that work to promote peace—tried to find a way. They called for disarmament, or getting rid of weapons. They also wanted a treaty to end all war. In 1928, many countries signed a pledge never to go to war with one another again.

In the 1920s, many people did not save money. Instead they borrowed money to invest in the stock market. They expected to earn fortunes with little work. But the stock market failed them. Its value rose too quickly, and then it collapsed.

The Great Depression hit in 1929. Millions of people lost money. Almost half of America's banks failed. Many people lost their jobs. By 1932, more than 20 percent of the U.S. population was unemployed. Those who had jobs made less money. Thousands lost their homes or farms because they could not pay their bills.

Photographer Dorothea Lange captured images of people suffering poverty in the United States.

Her famous photograph, called *Migrant Mother*, became an iconic symbol of the Great Depression.

Unemployed men line up to get food in Chicago.

BRINGING HOPE

*Franklin D. Roosevelt became president of the United States in 1933. Under his leadership, Congress passed sweeping **reforms**. The government did more to control banks and the stock market. Work programs helped the unemployed. A new Social Security Act provided financial help to the elderly, the unemployed, and people with disabilities.*

Franklin D. Roosevelt
March 4, 1933 – April 12, 1945

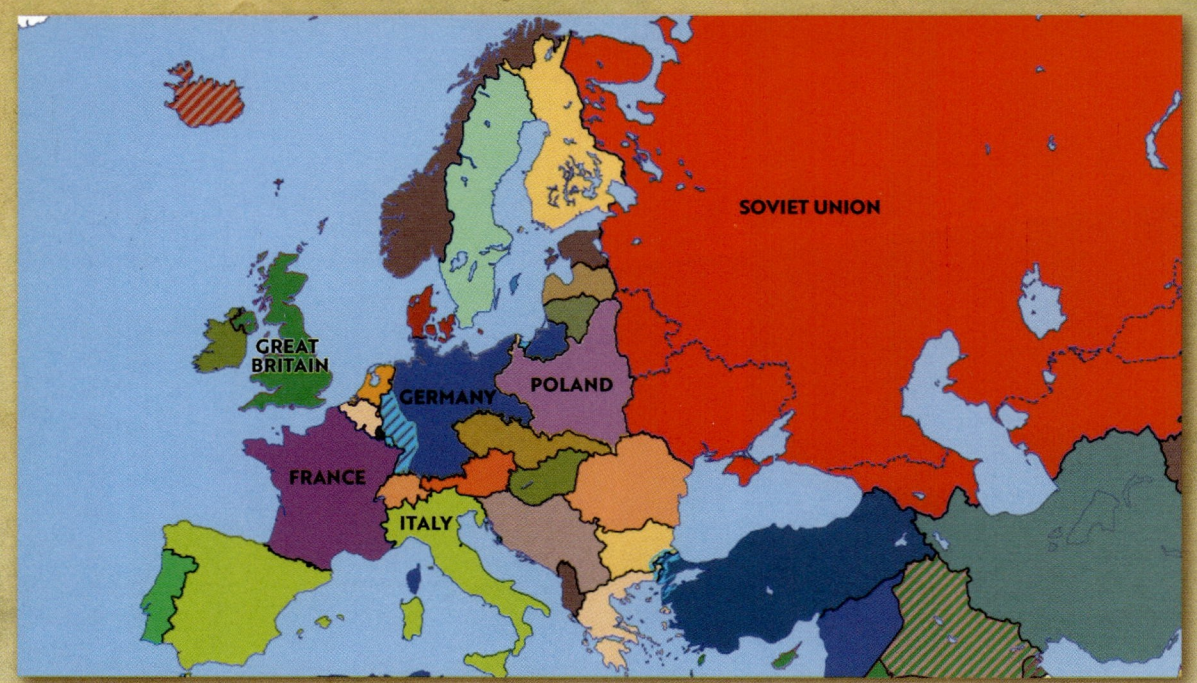

Map 1933

These economic problems spread throughout the world. The suffering led some people to join extreme political movements.

Germany suffered harsh penalties after losing World War I. Many Germans thought their humiliating defeat had caused the hard times. Misery and fear led to anger. People wanted drastic change to improve their lives.

Adolf Hitler promised this change. He promised to restore Germany to its "rightful position" as a world power. Under Hitler, the Nazis rose to power.

Adolf Hitler
April 20, 1889 – April 30, 1945

THE PARTY OF HATE

The Nazi party started small. It grew under Adolf Hitler, a powerful speaker. He was a master of propaganda, the use of biased information to promote a cause. He encouraged people to turn their anger and fear against certain groups. Jewish people were among those wrongly blamed for everyone's problems.

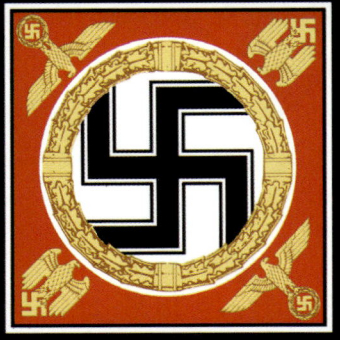

The swastika was used as a symbol for the Nazi party.

World War II began in 1939, when Germany invaded Poland. The U.S. stayed neutral at first. Most Americans did not want to get involved in another European war.

President Roosevelt thought Germany was clearly at fault in this conflict. He asked Congress to allow the sale of weapons to the Allies. Later, America loaned money to Great Britain. But the U.S. would not officially declare war—yet.

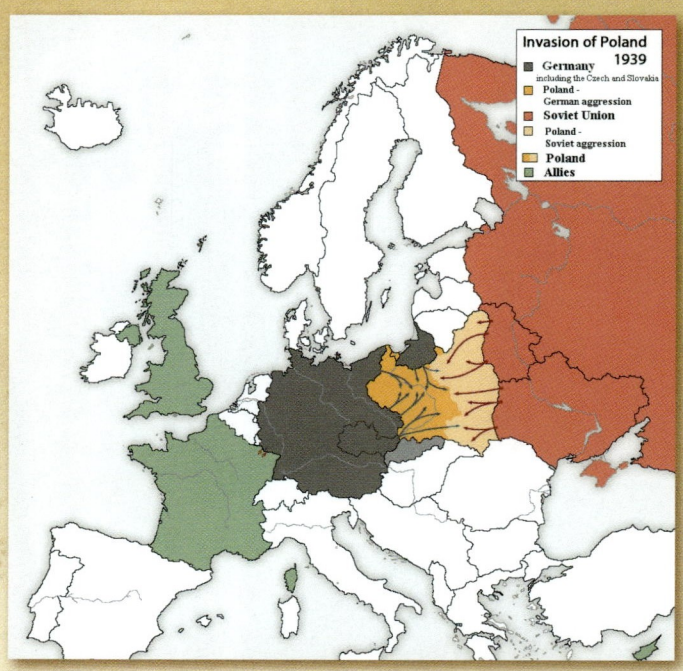

Germany invaded Poland in 1939.

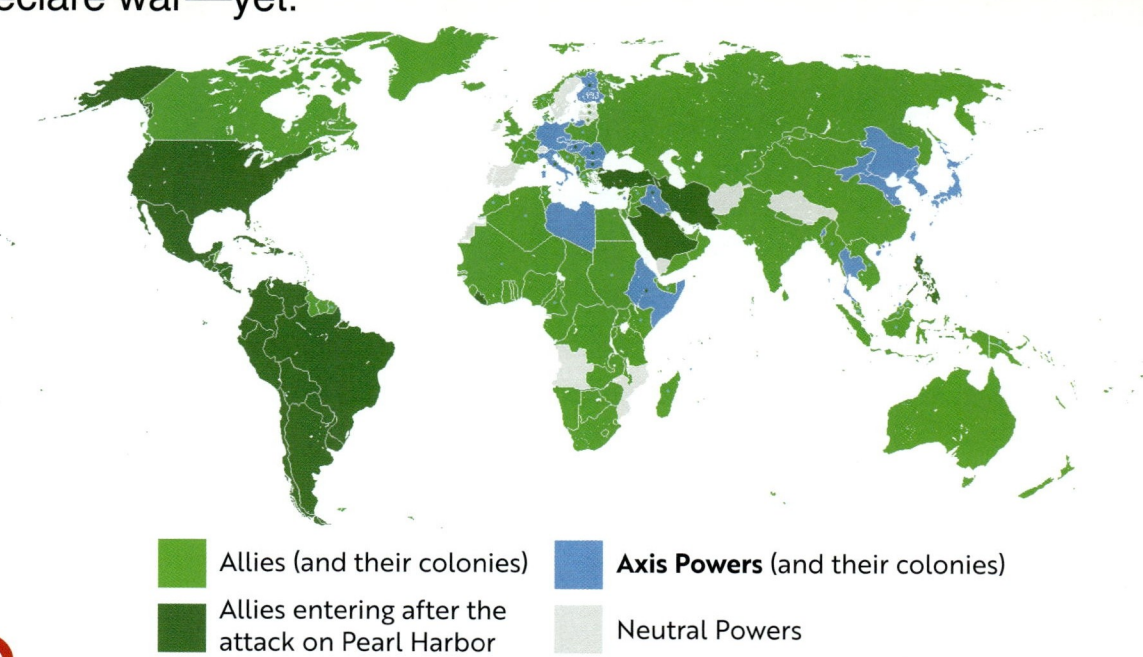

- Allies (and their colonies)
- Allies entering after the attack on Pearl Harbor
- **Axis Powers** (and their colonies)
- Neutral Powers

Still, the country began preparing. Factories made more weapons and other tools for defense. This created more jobs, helping the economy.

This New York factory made fighter aircraft.

ALLIES AND AXIS

World War II took place between two groups of countries. The Axis powers included Germany, Japan, and Italy. They wanted to take over more territory. The Allied powers, or Allies, included Great Britain, the United States, China, and the Soviet Union. Their goal was to defeat the Axis powers.

CHAPTER TWO

WAR BRINGS CHANGE

War came to America despite the efforts to avoid it. On December 7, 1941, the Japanese bombed Hawaii. The surprise attack hit the U.S. naval base at Pearl Harbor. Japan hoped to destroy the U.S. fleet there. More than 2,300 U.S. soldiers died.

Pearl Harbor is in Hawaii, on the island of Oahu.

A U.S. ship burns after the attack on Pearl Harbor.

This photo taken by a Japanese plane shows a torpedo strike on a U.S. battleship.

A U.S. battleship is destroyed during the attack.

A DAY OF INFAMY

*One day after the attack on Pearl Harbor, President Roosevelt delivered a speech. He called December 7, 1941, "a date which will live in **infamy**." He then asked the U.S. Congress to declare war with Japan.*

President Roosevelt signs the declaration of war against Japan.

The bombing of Pearl Harbor dragged America into the war. The American people united in their determination to fight. They would not let the enemy get away with this horror! Congress declared war on Japan. Soon it also declared war on the other Axis powers.

America was already recovering from the Depression. The billions spent on the war effort further helped the economy. Factories built ships, planes, and military vehicles. They made weapons and ammunition. These factories needed many new employees. Meanwhile, the military needed soldiers. Suddenly the country had enough work for everyone.

Women went to work as men headed to war.

America had not been making many weapons, but that changed quickly. Soon the country was making far more weapons than its enemies. The U.S. also developed new and better weapons. This helped the Allies win the war.

A U.S. factory makes bomber planes.

A test of the Manhattan Project. This was the first time a nuclear weapon was exploded.

THE MANHATTAN PROJECT

In 1939, scientists learned that Germany was working on a new weapon. This atomic bomb could cause incredible destruction. Scientists such as Albert Einstein had moved to America, fleeing the Nazi regime. He and others thought America needed its own bomb project. This project was given a code name: Manhattan Project.

America already had a reputation for innovation. The country also gained many new scientists who were fleeing danger in Europe. With a war underway, people worked hard to invent new products. Some of these would be important long after the war.

Engineers made the first computers for the Army. They also improved radio and radar devices. Government scientists made advances in television technology.

Edward Teller (1908 - 2003) came from Hungary. He helped the U.S. build the first atomic bomb.

THE COMPUTER AGE
Originally a "computer" was a person who made calculations. The earliest machine computers were powered by steam. In the 1930s, work on electronic computers increased. Early versions from the 1940s would fill a 20 by 40 foot (6 by 12 meter) room.

This early computer was used by the U.S. military.

WWII plastic canteen

WWII metal canteen

Plastic was invented in the early 1900s. During the war, the material was used widely by the military. Plastic could replace metal, which was scarce.

BURIED IN PLASTIC

*To support the war effort, companies built new factories to turn crude oil into plastic. After the war, those factories needed new ways to make money. They created many new products for everyday use. Now plastic is everywhere, from drink bottles to car parts. It has become a major **pollutant**.*

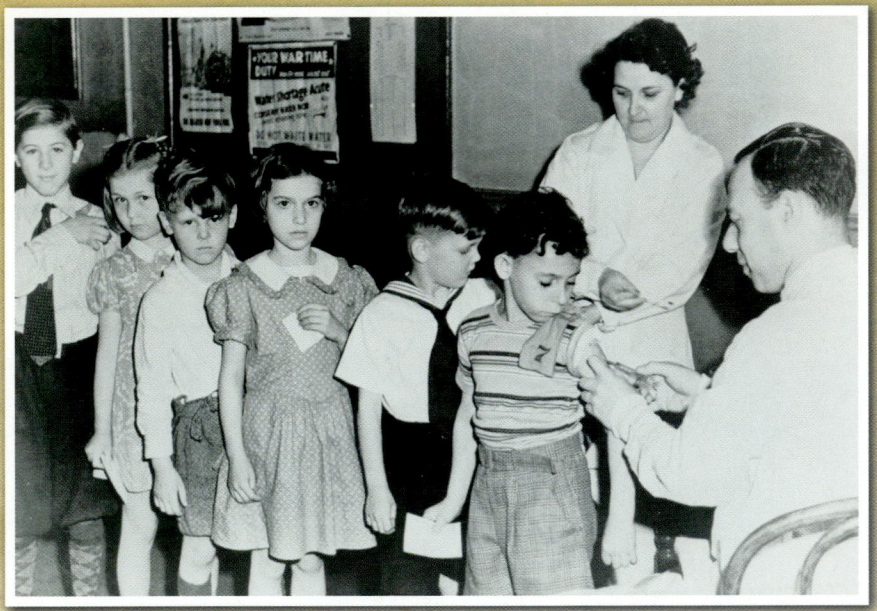
Children get shots to prevent diseases.

Science labs received more government funding. This helped them make great advances. Many new "wonder drugs" were developed. These included new antibiotics, drugs to fight infections. These drugs saved many lives during the war and in the years since.

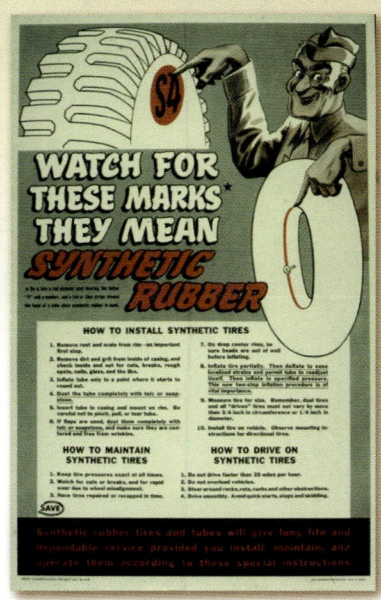
A poster from the 1940s advertises rubber tires.

Many groups worked together to solve problems. Tanks, airplanes, and battleships used rubber parts. Soldiers' clothing, shoes, and equipment contained rubber. Natural rubber mostly came from Southeast Asia. The war cut off this supply. American chemists scrambled to develop a substitute. The government, universities, and private companies worked together. They created a synthetic rubber. Most U.S. rubber is now synthetic.

The USS *Indianapolis* was sunk by Japanese torpedoes in 1945.

Only 317 of the nearly 1,200 men on board lived.

Children learn to help in the garden.

During the First World War, Americans planted "victory gardens." People could eat their home-grown food, saving farm products for the soldiers. During World War II, the government discouraged people from planting home gardens. They were afraid more food production would hurt farms. Still, within two years, America had 20 million victory gardens.

A poster promotes victory gardens.

THE ORIGINAL SPAM
Spam, a canned meat product, was introduced in the 1930s. It shipped easily and lasted for a long time. This made it an ideal food for soldiers in the field. The military used 15 million cans of Spam each week.

POWS IN THE FIELDS

With many young men at war, farms couldn't find workers. They began using captured prisoners. America housed over 400,000 prisoners of war (POWs). Many were allowed to work on farms and were paid for their work. Building POW camps also provided jobs for local workers.

The gardens turned out to be needed. Farms struggled to produce enough food. They couldn't get enough workers. Transportation problems made it hard to get food to stores. Fruits and vegetables were not always available to buy. Victory gardens helped keep people fed and healthy.

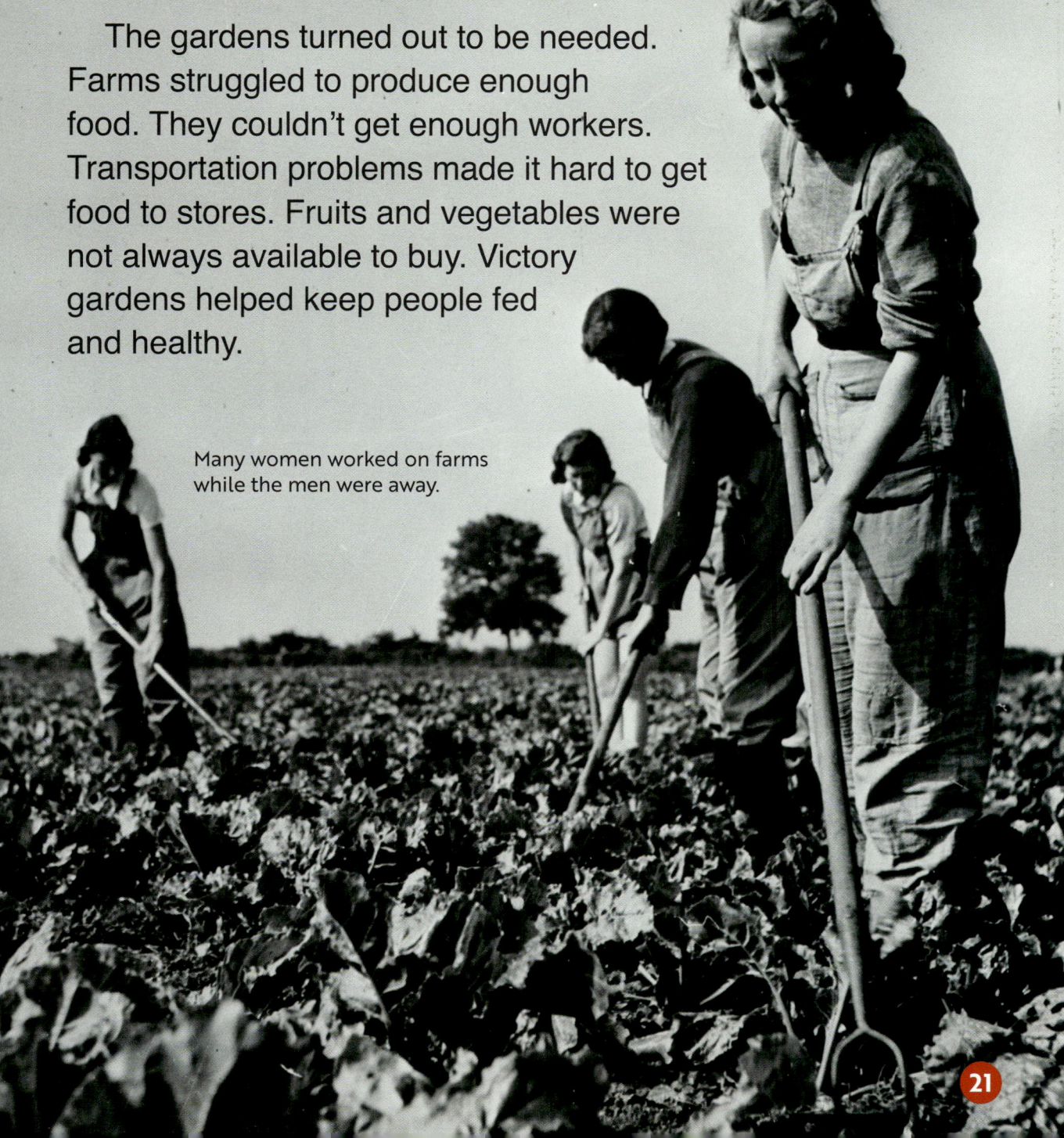

Many women worked on farms while the men were away.

RIGHTS EXPANDED, RIGHTS DESTROYED

Only men could fight, but women also went to war. Over 350,000 women volunteered for military service. Some joined because they wanted to help. Others wanted adventure or independence.

Many women served as nurses. They were allowed to do this work because women were seen as "natural caregivers." Other women in the military took on desk jobs so the men could fight. A **recruitment** poster told women, "Be A Marine. Free A Marine to Fight."

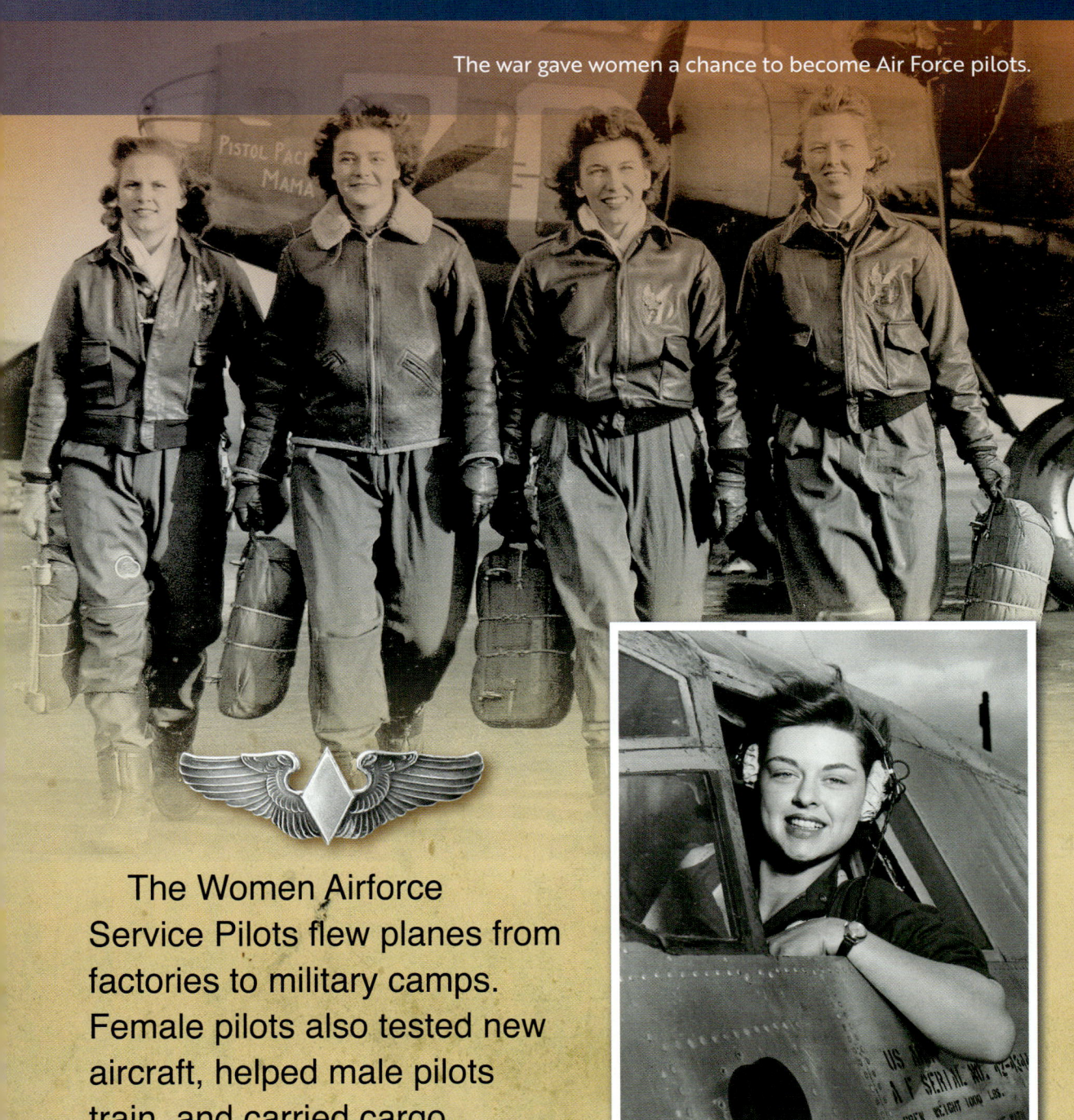

The war gave women a chance to become Air Force pilots.

The Women Airforce Service Pilots flew planes from factories to military camps. Female pilots also tested new aircraft, helped male pilots train, and carried cargo.

FEMININE ENOUGH?

Not everyone approved of women in the military. Some felt that "mannish" behavior was dangerous. Army women were told "to avoid rough or masculine appearance." They had to prove they could still be traditional women.

Women work in a factory in 1942.

Millions more women took jobs back home. They did work previously done by men. They became mechanics and welders. They worked in factories and on farms. They took jobs in offices, banks, and stores.

A woman working on aircraft in California in 1942.

An ad asks women to join the workforce.

EQUAL PAY?

*Federal rules required equal pay for similar work. However, women earned less than men. In 1944, skilled female workers earned an average of $31.21 per week. Men in similar jobs earned $54.65 per week. Still, new war **industry** jobs paid much better than previous jobs available to women.*

Society still expected women to care for their homes and children. Often stores were only open while women were at work. That made shopping difficult. Childcare was nearly impossible to find. Meanwhile, women of color faced racism. Some were **harassed** and even physically attacked at work.

A public nursery for the children of U.S. war workers.

Women welders in 1943.

HELPING WORKING WOMEN

*To lure women into the workforce, the government **mandated** certain supports. For example, women were supposed to have access to daycare for their children. However, the supply of daycare did not meet the demand. After the war, many employers cut the benefits that had appealed to women.*

Women who moved to big cities or military sites had more freedom. Parents and neighbors no longer watched and controlled their movements. Women talked more about their desires. Gay women had new chances to socialize and fall in love.

An early photo of movie star Marilyn Monroe (1926 - 1962).

QUICK MARRIAGE, QUICK DIVORCE

Marriage rates rose during the war. Some women feared husbands would be hard to find with men at war. Couples often married quickly, before the men had to leave. Quick marriages and long-distance relationships led to high divorce rates.

Women also faced more harassment. Men whistled and shouted rude comments at them on the street. Women who moved to cities often had trouble finding housing. Many had to live in crowded boarding houses. Women living alone were viewed with suspicion. Those who grabbed wartime opportunities to improve their own lives were seen as selfish. They should be helping the war effort, not themselves.

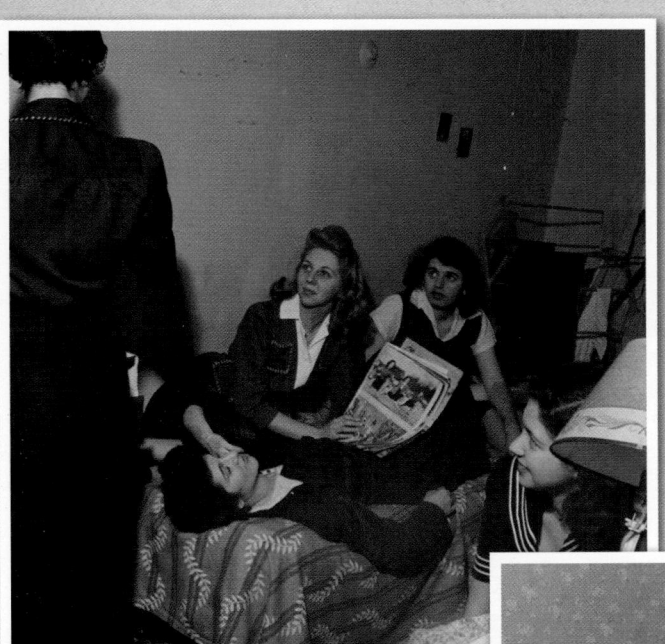

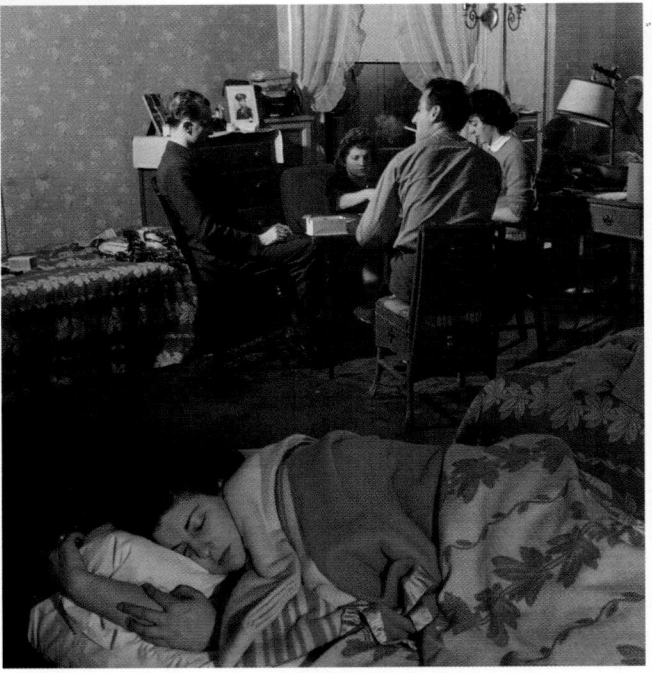

A boarding house in Washington, D.C., in the 1940s.

Racism affected every aspect of American society before the war. The need for wartime workers encouraged some changes. President Roosevelt made an Executive Order that banned discrimination in defense industries. This widened the range of occupations available to African Americans.

An African-American woman works on a bomber plane.

A bus station in North Carolina had separate areas for African Americans in the 1940s.

RACE RIOTS

Some white Americans feared the changing racial mix in their cities. Meanwhile, minorities were demanding more rights. This led to violent race riots in cities from Los Angeles to New York. Sometimes white soldiers, sailors, and police officers began the riots.

Many African Americans had already been moving from the South to the North. This movement increased as workers sought new jobs. In the 1940s, over one million African Americans moved to cities in the West and Northeast. They found new opportunities, but they still faced discrimination. Many cities forced different races to live in separated areas.

Some groups had better opportunities during the war. Yet, World War II also saw one of the greatest civil rights violations in U.S. history. The Japanese living in America were feared as spies. Over 110,000 Japanese Americans were imprisoned. They were sent to **internment** camps, often in remote areas.

Children in California pledge allegiance to the U.S. flag in 1942.

The president's wife, Eleanor Roosevelt (1884 - 1962), visits an internment camp.

An internment camp in Wyoming.

LOYAL AMERICANS

At first Japanese Americans were not allowed to join the armed forces. In 1943, the government changed its policy. Japanese Americans could join special segregated army units. Thousands volunteered. Many wanted to prove they were loyal Americans. Their unit became known for extraordinary bravery.

Two thirds of the prisoners were U.S. citizens. Many had spent their entire lives in America. Not a single case of spying was blamed on a Japanese American. Americans of German or Italian descent were not sent to camps.

An internment camp in California.

YOU CAN'T GO HOME AGAIN

The last internment camp closed in 1946. Many Japanese Americans had lost their businesses, farms, and homes. They still faced suspicion and discrimination.

In 1988, U.S. President Ronald Reagan (1911 - 2004) signed a law that gave money to Japanese Americans who had been in the camps.

The Nazis murdered millions of Jewish people. This horror is now known as the Holocaust. U.S. papers reported on some of this violence. However, they did not always note that the victims were Jewish. Most Americans did not understand the full impact of the Holocaust until much later.

Jewish people captured by Germans in Poland.

NEVER FORGET

Today the Holocaust is remembered around the world. Many countries and U.S. states have Holocaust museums or monuments. These places help people remember what happens when we do not stand up for victims of persecution.

The U.S. Holocaust Memorial Museum in Washington, D.C.

Refugees at a shelter in New York.

In 1939 and 1940, more than half of all immigrants to the U.S. were Jewish. Most immigrants came from countries under Nazi threat. Still, many Jewish refugees were not admitted, even if they were fleeing from the Nazis. America had strong limits on immigration. The war did not change that.

Ellis Island, New York, was a major entry for immigrants.

The war brought new freedom to some groups. At the same time, the government controlled many aspects of daily life. The president banned pleasure drives as a waste of gas. He had the right to make sweeping decisions if they were "useful" to the war effort.

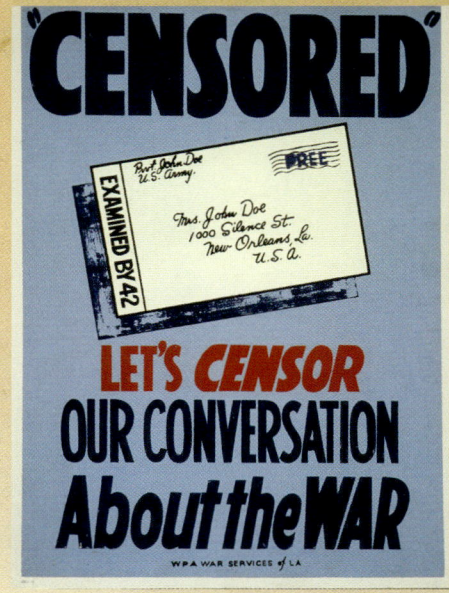

Military **censors** could open and read every letter that entered or left the country. A letter from a soldier might reach home with entire paragraphs cut out. The censors could also screen every phone call. This was partly to prevent the sharing of military secrets. It was also to limit bad news and maintain support for the war.

Cars line up in Des Moines, Iowa.

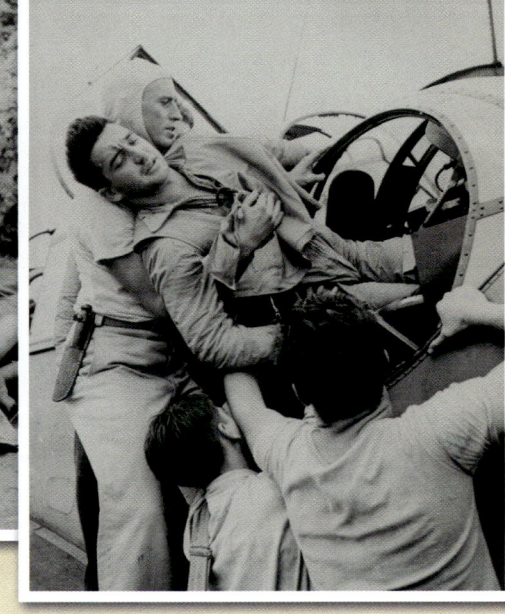

A soldier gets medical help in 1943.

DEATH AT THE DOOR

The government and media could not hide the deaths of soldiers. People dreaded the arrival of a telegram. This little piece of paper often carried a terrible message. It might say a family member had been wounded or killed or was missing in action.

Arlington National Cemetery, a military cemetery in Virginia.

Americans got most of their war news through the media. Newspapers and radio broadcasts reported on the war. In theaters, the news played before the movies. The government controlled all this news.

U.S. troops wade through water as Germans shoot at them.

Reporters shared inspiring stories about the war effort. Reports of combat focused on the positive: All U.S. soldiers were reported to be brave and heroic. All leaders were cast as smart and noble. People at home were protected from the harsh realities of war.

Soldiers in battle.

At first the media could not share images of dead American soldiers. That changed in the fall of 1943. Almost two years had passed since the attack on Pearl Harbor. The public was weary of war and losing interest. The government allowed LIFE magazine to publish a photo of dead U.S. soldiers. Later, the War Department released a film showing brutal fighting. They hoped to rally more support for the war effort.

The Iwo Jima Memorial is dedicated to all marines who have given their lives in battle.

THE GOOD WAR

Even today, America's actions in World War II are often seen as morally correct. Films usually portray American soldiers as heroic and patriotic. The audience can root for the heroes as they destroy the enemy. Films about the Vietnam War, on the other hand, often show the horrors of war.

CHAPTER FOUR

SUFFERING AND SURVIVING

No matter how honorable the cause, war leads to suffering. Soldiers had to deal with loneliness, boredom, and fear. Thousands suffered from mental illness after they returned home. These people were supposed to be the strongest and fittest of all. Yet they could still have breakdowns.

WHAT ARE YOU FIGHTING FOR?
Some soldiers fought for ideals. Others only wanted to return to normal life. One veteran said, "To get home, you had to end the war. To end the war was the reason you fought it. The only reason."

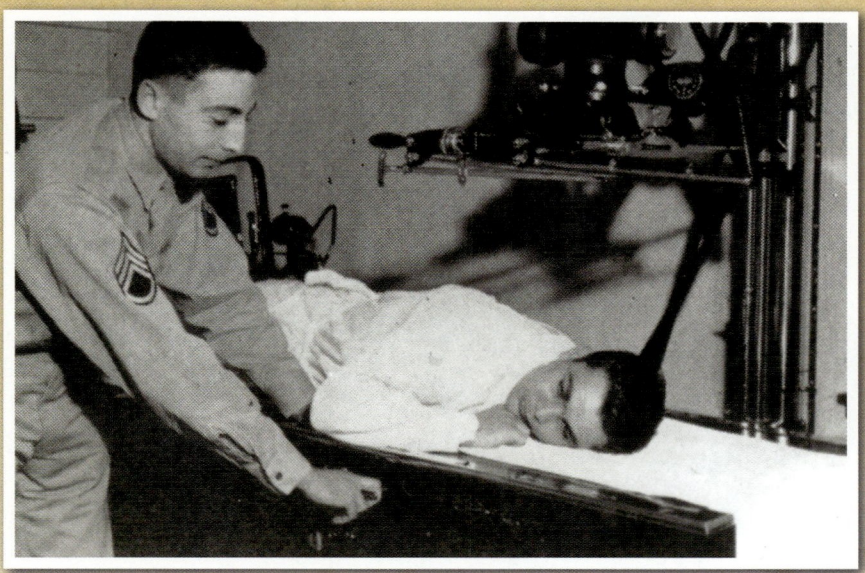

A military hospital in California.

American doctors gained a new understanding of mental health. Mental illness wasn't a weakness or something people were born with. Anyone might suffer the effects of extreme stress. This realization led to new treatments.

A U.S. military hospital during WWII.

MENTAL HEALTH

Before World War II, most mentally ill people went to hospitals. They might live there for life. After the war, people started to see mental health as important for everyone. People could seek help while continuing their normal lives.

On August 6, 1945, a U.S. plane dropped an atomic bomb on Japan. Three days later, the U.S. dropped a second bomb. Two Japanese cities were destroyed. More than 150,000 people died instantly. Thousands more died in the following months from the effects of the bombs.

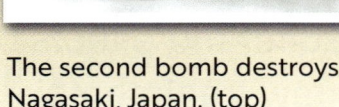

The second bomb destroys Nagasaki, Japan. (top)

A model of the atomic bomb.

A famous photo taken at the end of the war. (right)

PROMOTING PEACE

After World War I, the League of Nations was formed. This international organization tried to promote peace by giving countries a forum for resolving disputes. This failed to prevent World War II. The Allies then agreed to establish a stronger international group. The United Nations supports cooperation between countries. This has not ended all war. Still, we have not had another worldwide war.

Japanese officials arrive on a U.S. ship to formally surrender.

BASIC RIGHTS

In 1948, the United Nations proclaimed a standard for all people in all countries. The Universal Declaration of Human Rights sets out basic human rights that should be protected. It states, "Everyone has the right to life, liberty and security of person."

Photos from August 1945 show the results of the bomb on Hiroshima.

These bombs killed ordinary people as well as soldiers. The bombings have been called a crime against **humanity**. They have also been called moral and fair. Dropping the bombs saved American lives. Japanese lives would also have been lost had the war continued. We can never know whether the bombs saved more lives than they ended.

CHAPTER FIVE

LINGERING EFFECTS

The years after the war are often called the "postwar era." Many changes came to America. Men came home from fighting and needed jobs. New housing developments with identical homes sprang up around cities. Families moved to these suburbs. They bought cars so men could commute to work.

A highway under construction in Mississippi.

This 1957 Chevrolet was one of many new cars to hit the roads.

ROADS AND SUBURBS

The interstate highway system was built to help men find and keep jobs. They could work in city centers and live in suburbs. Along with roads came shopping malls, motels, fast food, and drive-in theaters.

Suburbs in Pennsylvania.

During the war, women kept busy at home, shopping, and on the job.

Society expected women to stay in the home. They were encouraged to embrace the role of wife and mother. New devices such as refrigerators and vacuum cleaners helped with housework.

Some women returned to their old roles with relief. Others were not willing to give up their new freedoms. They had proven they could do the same skilled work as men. They still struggled to convince employers.

SMOKE AND FOG

More factories and more cars also meant more pollution. In 1943, Los Angeles suffered its first attack of smog. Smog is fog or haze combined with smoke and other pollutants. This air pollution harms people's health. It remained a major problem until the 1970s. Then environmental regulations helped reduce pollution.

Joseph Stalin (1878 - 1953) was a Communist dictator in the Soviet Union.

World War II led to a new kind of war: the Cold War. The U.S. and the Soviet Union (Russia) were at odds. The U.S. promoted capitalism, a system where private companies control trade and industry. The Soviet Union was founded on communism. In this system, property is owned by the government.

Stalin, Roosevelt, and British Prime Minister Winston Churchill meet.

NO LONGER PRISONERS
Prisoners of war came from Germany, Italy, Japan, and other Axis countries. Most went back to their home countries by 1946. A few decided to stay and become American citizens.

Americans were afraid communism would destroy the country. It was a threat to "the American Way." One's neighbor or coworker might be a communist. Fear brought people together: fear of the "commie" in their midst.

World War II is often referred to as "The Good War." America fought a terrible evil and kept Nazis from taking over the world. Soldiers and citizens defended American civilization and values. The war effort also improved the economy. This put an end to the Great Depression.

A flyer warns against communism.

Yet this war was as full of horror as any other, and its long-term effects varied. Women took a step toward equality and then were forced back. In the post-war era, minorities still faced racism. Rich and poor were still greatly divided. The future would see more people insisting on rights: women's rights, civil rights, workers' rights, and gay and lesbian rights.

It is worth remembering the horrors of World War II, from the Holocaust to the bombings. They carry a great lesson: We must prevent such wars in the future.

INVASION!

Movies of the 1940s and 1950s took advantage of the fear of outsiders. Many showed aliens invading the Earth. In Invasion of the Body Snatchers, aliens take over people's bodies. This played on the fear that one's neighbor might be a secret communist.

GLOSSARY

censors (SEN-sers): officials who examine letters from soldiers or prisoners in order to delete information considered a threat to security

harassed (hu-RASSD): repeatedly disturbed or tormented

humanity (hyu-MAE-nih-ti): the race of human beings

industry (IN-duh-stri): the process of turning raw materials into finished goods, or companies that do this

infamy (IN-fuh-mi): evil or shameful reputation

internment (ihn-TUHRN-mihnt): prison, especially those camps used during wartime

mandated (MAN-date-ed): authorized or required by law

pollutant (puh-LUTE-ent): something that makes air, water, or land unhealthy

recruitment (rih-KRUT-ment): the act of getting people to join the armed forces or another group

reforms (rih-FORMS): the improvements of bad conditions, especially through political action

segregated (SE-gruh-GAY-tihd): separated by race or ethnicity

INDEX

allies   10, 11, 15, 40
axis   10, 11, 13, 44
Communism   44, 45
food production   20
Franklin D. Roosevelt   7, 10, 13, 28, 44
Germany   8, 9, 10, 11, 15, 44
Holocaust   32, 45
immigrants   33
internment camps   30, 31
inventions   16, 17, 18, 19
postwar era   42
prisoners of war   21, 44
racism   25, 28, 45
The Great Depression   6, 14, 45
weapons   5, 10, 11, 14, 15
women   14, 22, 23, 24, 25, 26, 27, 43, 45

SHOW WHAT YOU KNOW

1. Why did America refuse to get involved in World War II at first?
2. Why did America finally join the war?
3. How did the war affect Japanese Americans?
4. How did the war affect African Americans?
5. How did the war change the role of women in American society?

FURTHER READING

Adams, Simon, *DK Eyewitness Books: World War II*, DK Children, 2014.

Gitlin, Martin, *World War II on the Home Front: An Interactive History Adventure*, Capstone Press, 2012.

Frank, Anne, *Anne Frank: The Diary of a Young Girl*, Bantam reissue edition, 1993.

ABOUT THE AUTHOR

M. M. Eboch writes fiction and nonfiction for all ages, but historical novels are her favorite. Her books for young people include *An Artful Escape, Walking the Dragon's Back,* and *The Well of Sacrifice.* She lives in New Mexico with her husband and their two ferrets.

© 2019 Rourke Educational Media

All rights reserved. No part of this book may be reproduced or utilized in any form or by any means, electronic or mechanical including photocopying, recording, or by any information storage and retrieval system without permission in writing from the publisher.

www.rourkeeducationalmedia.com

Photo Credits: Cover courtesy of U.S. Government; Page4-5 courtesy Don Troiani https://creativecommons.org/licenses/by/2.0/deed.en , peace sign By 1000 Words Shutterstock.com, dove sketch By Hadrian Shutterstock.com; Page6-7 migrant mother and family of three photos courtesy of Library of Congress, line outside soup kitchen and Roosevelt courtesy of National Archives; Page8-9 Hitler courtesy of German Federal Archive, map By lynx_v Shutterstock.com; Page10-11 aircraft factory courtesy Library of Congress, map Listowy at English Wikipedia.; Page12-13 a burning USS Arizona courtesy National Archives, USS West Virginia photos courtesy Library of Congress and U.S. Navy, map By Peter Hermes Furian Shutterstock.com, Roosevelt courtesy U.S. Government; page14-15 woman factory worker Courtesy National Archives, planes courtesy of U.S. Air Force, Trinity Test courtesy U.S. Dept of Energy. Page16-17; gilotyna, hedgehog94, US.gov, Courtsey Library Of Congress-Public Domain. Page18-19; United States Department of the Treasury, U.S.O.W.I., U.S. Navy. Page20-21; Morley. USDA, Rosener, Ann, U.S.O.W.I., Library Of Congress-Public Domain. Page22-23; us.mil, Australian Copyright Council-Fair Use—Government, USAF. Page24-25; US-Farm Security Admin., Bramley, Maurice (Department of National Service), Bransby, David-Library Of Congress-Public Domain, The US National Archives. Page26-27; Teichnor Bros, Library Of Congress-Public Domain. Page28-29; Alfred T Palmer -Library Of Congress, Courtsey Library Of Congress-Public Domain. Page30-31; Dorothea Lang, Roosevelt Presidential Library, rypson-istock.com, Ronald Reagan Presidential library. Page32-33; CC0 1.0 Universal Public Domain Dedication, Ken Thomas, The US National Archives. Page34-35; John Vachon, DarkN8, The US National Archives. Page36-37; Robert F. Sargent, Lt. Robert Fields. (KIA), Smith, Dan V, www.defensemedianetwork.com. Page38-39; USAF, Courtesy Library Of Congress-Public Domain. Page40-41; mil.gov, US Navy. Page42-43; O'Halloran, J. Thomas, Ann Rosener, The US National Archives. Page44-45; US Signal Corp, Library Of Congress-Public Domain. Page46-47; tankbmb, csfotoimages, Acoll123.

Edited by: Keli Sipperley

Produced by Blue Door Education for Rourke Educational Media. Cover and Interior design by: Jennifer Dydyk

Living Through World War II / M. M. Eboch
(American Culture and Conflict)
  ISBN 978-1-64156-417-5 (hard cover)
  ISBN 978-1-64156-543-1 (soft cover)
  ISBN 978-1-64156-666-7 (e-Book)
Library of Congress Control Number: 2018930437

Rourke Educational Media
Printed in the United States of America, North Mankato, Minnesota